I0502818

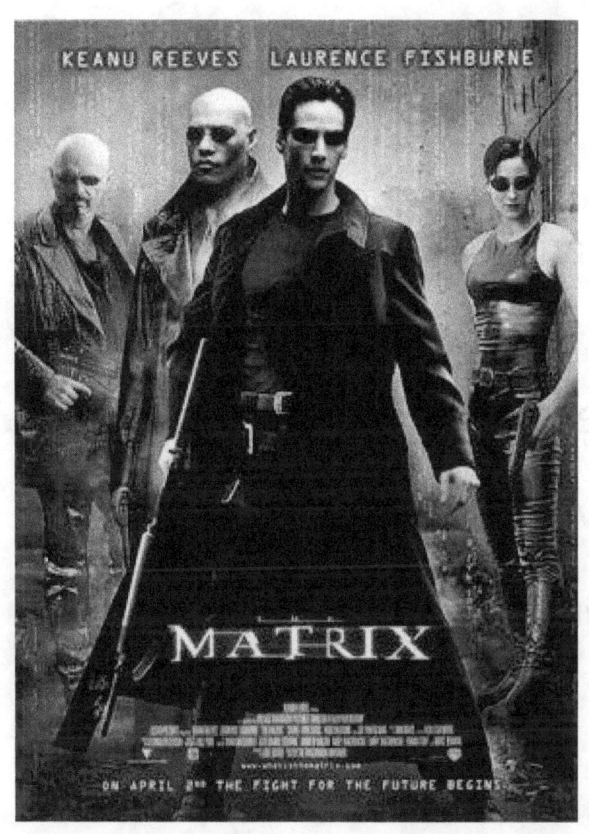

The Matrix (the movie series) – An Analysis

Contents

1. Introduction

The movie series of The Matrix was another powerhouse production, made by the Wachowski brothers. There were similar scenarios in the movie, with plenty of action and heroes and heroines, but also something different with a number of metaphors functioning to make The Matrix a memorable one. Even the title, The Matrix, had some special hidden aura to it. For action and special effects, The Matrix was one of the best all time favourite movies, and the amount of time, energy and money that went into such a movie had better produce something special...and it did. Neo's (Keanu Reeves) battles with Agent Smith (Hugo Weaving) were unbelievable and were what made The Matrix all the more better and memorable.

However, Neo and Agent Smith reverse roles of good guy-bad guy at various times in the movie series as both have good points, as well as bad points. Action was definitely the main ingredient in The Matrix, but if a viewer held on the other themes and elements come through beautifully. An animation series and video game were also made as supports to and follows on to

The Matrix. There are seven themes in The Matrix that are directly and indirectly communicated to the audience: 'The Hero and Heroine', 'Good versus Bad', 'Religion', 'Family', 'Action', 'Love', 'Image', 'Technology and Science'. Each of these themes will be looked at and analysed in the report.

2. Brief Description

The Matrix was definitely a future-based Science-Fiction thriller. It did come across as somewhat dark, for example the black outfits most of the cast were wearing. More movies nowadays are being future-based, as if people want to know what is going to happen in the future, which is only natural and makes perfect common sense; as the saying goes, 'Failing to Plan is Planning to Fail'. Movies like The Matrix provide a medium to let out and communicate these thoughts and feelings about such things as the future, technology and how we will live and function.

Movies these days are also Science-Fiction based, as a lot of our society is based around science, for example, medicine, health, technology and new products and services. Again, such scenarios are combined with

Action of some sort, whether it is military of some sort, weapons or hand-to-hand combat, to liven up the movie. Of course, the presence of some or a lot of action in the movie is aimed at men, especially younger males from 15 years of age to 30-35 years of age, as this is the prime time for a young male.

The Matrix seemed to be labelled and sectioned-off as another future-based, Science Fiction film, with dark connotations. This meant it would have suited some people but not all people. But, news of this blockbuster spread to others and it began to catch on. Having a series of movies for The Matrix made it more appealing as it extended the Action and storyline even further and left viewers wanting more, almost like a James Bond 007, Bourne Ultimatum series or Jet Li or Jackie Chan martial arts movies. However, as mentioned, the Action and special effects, the use of some metaphors, a wellput-together cast and script and a big budget, came through in the film to make it a blockbuster.

The Wachowski brothers went through a lot of time and effort to make this film, and it will always be a masterpiece for them in their eyes and viewers the world over and movie-world itself. For example, The Matrix won several awards for various elements in the series of films, like best hero and villain in Neo and Agent Smith respectively. But as stated earlier, both Neo and Agent Smith are both good and bad in their approaches, and this will be analysed later under Themes.

3. Themes

The Hero and Heroine

The Matrix has a hero and heroine at the same time in Neo and Trinity. It is like Superman and Wonder Woman or Batman and Catwoman. Actually the latter resembles Neo and Trinity based on the outfits they wear. Neo helps Trinity as Trinity helps Neo, a perfect duo, with the help of Morpheus, another hero in the picture. Neo saves Trinity's life on a number of occasions, like after meeting the maker of The Matrix, and Trinity saves his when the Agent tries to shoot him on the rooftop. Trinity is an amazing woman to be able to keep up with Neo, despite Neo being on another level to everyone.

Neo and Trinity resemble the Merovingian and his wife Persephone, who they meet in later Matrix movies. The

Merovingian used to be like Neo, and has encountered similar Ones like Neo before. The Merovingian did not seem too worried about Neo, but of course, was more concerned about the Key Master he had captured. It would have been an interesting battle if Neo battled The Merovingian, who was more on his level. Persephone did not seem like the fighting type, although this remains to be seen, not wearing your typical combat outfit, but coming across as typically feminine.

Good versus Bad

Neo and Agent Smith reverse roles throughout the film in a good-bad, bad-good relationship. Neo is seen as the anti-Hero, standing up against authority in the form of Agent Smith. They resemble feuding brothers, friends or a father and son relationship going back and forth. If it had to be one or the other who is correct, it would have to be Agent Smith. On several occasions he tries to reason with Neo, but Neo continues doing what he does, because, 'he chooses to...' Smith makes a valid comment how 'humans just multiply' and they, as part of The Matrix, 'were the cure'. What Agent Smith was trying to say is that humanity, in fact nature, does need a helping hand. Things may have fallen apart in the world if those from The Matrix had not helped out humanity and allowed people to function freely.

In stating this, it would be difficult for Zion in The Matrix to cope with humans multiplying freely. What space would there be and would there be some form of birth control? But Morpheus and the Zion crew were also correct in that those in The Matrix tried to copy and take over humans, for example, when Agent Smith said,

'…we tried to copy your species, but at first it failed, and whole crops were lost'. Crops, since when were humans' crops. This is where science and technology go too far, as is a typical theme in most future-based and or science fiction movies these days. Agent Smith does a role reversal with Neo by becoming the thing that he hated so much, a criminal, but he does not realise this and thinks he is doing the right thing. Agent Smith tries to take over The Matrix by taking over people by force and making them be like him. Neo therefore becomes the good guy and hero, not only for Zion, but also for The Matrix by aiming to stop Agent Smith.

However, Neo does have a case in that people do have a free will and that people should not be targeted for being different and living their lives. Neo and the crew were humanitarians in one way, trying to save Zion and those in it, but so was Agent Smith in that he was supporting life and the people in The Matrix, for example when he first met Neo and stated, 'one life [as Neo] was not needed, and that he would wipe the slate clean and have Anderson continue or start a new life. But Neo wanted to know about The Matrix more than anything.

It was the way Neo and the rest of the Zion crew have gone about it that was the problem. One might say if Neo had not done what he had done, he may never have met the maker of The Matrix in the way he did and ultimately saved Zion. What Agent Smith was trying to say is that there is a better and proper way. Anderson was also guilty of many cyber-crimes, which has no excuses and what some people, young and old, are doing today, amongst other crimes. Perhaps there was a breaking point in Neo, who had had enough, and probably needed some help and assistance. Cybercrime was not the way to go. Neo was bored, lonely and depressed, so when given a chance, he took his rebellion to a higher level through Morpheus and being given a chance to find out what The Matrix was about.

Morpheus was also to blame, and Cipher was right to an extent, in that Morpheus was putting these so called free peoples' lives at risk by having them physically fight authority, especially Agents. Neo's adverse reaction to Morpheus explanation about The Matrix, i.e. flipping out, supported his initial rejection of The Matrix, supporting Cipher's hidden anger towards Morpheus for taking him out of The Matrix.

What Morpheus was really trying to do was save Zion, the hidden space under the Earth out of The Matrix. This is what he really wanted Neo to do. Surely Morpheus and The Oracle could have pulled some strings and had a peaceful demonstration to authorities, the Agents including Smith and especially the maker of the Matrix to save Zion. But no, Neo had to go through all that he went through. Of course this was a movie and is makebelieve so there was going to be a different method to get to authority. In this sense, Neo is good for wanting to save Zion and Agent Smith is good for trying to keep order and support life in The Matrix. But Neo is bad for rebelling very negatively through physical force and pushing too far with wanting to find out about The Matrix and his love for Trinity.

Religion

Religion is a major theme in The Matrix. The mentioning of the rebels hidden base away from The Matrix as titled, Zion. Zion was stated in the Bible in the Old Testament. Zion could represent in The Matrix a hidden sanctuary or paradise, in this case away from The Matrix, i.e. the world. The actual physical premises of Zion resembled like that of Hell. Perhaps Zion in The Matrix was a blend of Heaven and Hell. In this reality, it would be a reasonable question to state whether there was a Heaven for these people, or if they believed in a Heaven. Morpheus' aircraft ship was called the Nebuchadnezzar, another term used in the Old Testament with King Nebuchadnezzar, who was having dreams of being overthrown and was in fact a cruel king. Probably Morpheus' ship was a metaphor for The Matrix or using a bit of their own medicine.

Anderson, who becomes Neo, is said to be like a Christlike presence for the inhabitants of Zion, and later for The Matrix, by taking on the powers that be for the common good. There is even a miracle when he magically revives Trinity after being shot by the Agent after almost falling to her death. Morpheus called Neo, The One, as in the one to probably rescue Zion. Neo is a blend of Moses and Jesus. Neo is like Moses in that he used some force to take on The Matrix, like Moses used the force of God to defeat the Egyptians with the plagues. Neo is like Jesus in that he used himself and his skill and ability to take on The Matrix. It was Neo's love for Trinity, love for those in Zion, and as the story of the movie progressed, his love for those in The Matrix, just like Jesus and Moses had love.

Of course Morpheus pumped in 10 hours' worth of information into Neo's mind, which was a metaphor for the Holy Spirit bestowing the knowledge upon him. A normal person would not usually take in this amount of information like Neo did. The science and technology of The Matrix would have pushed the boundaries of humanity too far to some extent, and this is what those in Zion were fighting against, as mentioned under 'Good versus Bad' theme. Birth control, yes, humans as crops, or storage devices, no. But then again the brain is a storage device, and people have different levels of taking in and understanding information.

Action

Action was the driving force behind The Matrix; it is what made the movie and series. The action was not your usual type of action, it was slowed down, sped up, taken all over town such as Trinity being chased in the beginning and Neo being chased after his first clash with Agent Smith in the original movie. The Matrix was known for its special effects and supreme martial arts action. Remember, Neo had been pumped with 10 hours worth of information, predominantly 'combat training'. Neo probably needed all of this to even come close to matching it with the Agents. But again, a peaceful resolution should have been searched for first with the main emphasis to save and protect Zion, and even have these inhabitants of Zion still be allowed to be part of The Matrix, as long as they behave.

Neo's clashes with Agent Smith were amongst the best fighting scenes ever, even with the special affects for example in the beginning of Matrix Reloaded after consulting The Oracle. Neo remained a one man band while Agent Smith just multiplied. Agent Smith always had the power, especially as major arms of the law in The Matrix. While others, even Morpheus could not fight off Agent Smith taking over their bodies, Neo managed to fight him off. Neo gives hope that we can also beat the computer at some stage.

It was remarked that Neo moved like the Agents to an extent, for example his initial sparring session with Morpheus in the beginning of the original Matrix and on the rooftop being shot at by an Agent. At that point, it was close but not enough to the calibre of an Agent. It was the love, as shown through Trinity and a metaphor for the healing and fulfilling love of God for us that set Neo free and put all the information in his head into working sense. Morpheus was like the opposite of an Obi-Wan Kenobi in Star Wars. Whereas Obi-Wan Kenobi tried to stop Anakin, later Darth Vader from going too far with his love for power, Morpheus encouraged and influenced Neo to be powerful, putting hours of knowledge in his head.   This   supports   Cipher's resentment at Morpheus for supposedly freeing him from The Matrix.

Love

Another main theme in The Matrix is Love. Neo and Trinity are the hero and heroine together on the surface, but also lovers deep down. Remember it was Trinity's love, or God's love, that saved Neo when Agent Smith had killed him at the end in the first movie in the series. It was Trinity's or God's love that kept Neo going right through the movie series and his journey. For example Neo stating to Trinity that he needed her in Matrix Revolutions. Perhaps Neo needed Trinity more so than she needed him. This is indicative of the fact that women can be a stronger sex too, for example, emotionally and dealing with pain, i.e. childbirth and periods or menstruation. But either way, there was that love there. It would be an interesting argument whether it was Trinity's or God's love or his hours of knowledge in his head that pushed Neo to do what he did in The Matrix. It was probably a combination of both.

This love was similar to a husband and wife traditionally and in the modern era. Neo was the hero but also stereotypically the bread-winner, going through the obstacles and challenges of life, in this case, The Matrix and Agent Smith, while Trinity was stereotypically the wife, keeping herself occupied doing other things. However Neo and Trinity also represented couples in the modern era because both were technically working, or in this case, in The Matrix. But both were usually sideby-side, which is like working at the same business, either their own or someone else's, or financially free and doing what they would like to do together.

However, Persephone, wife of the Merovingian, had experienced this love with the Merovingian when he was like Neo and wanted this feeling again. Persephone stated how this love was short-lived, in that it was, because it was too deep and powerful. The thing is, Neo and Trinity could have been like the Merovingian and Persephone and persuaded and or put aside to be in their love in peace, but Neo and Trinity were fighting to save Zion, which was the bigger issue to be dealt with.

Family

The inhabitants of Zion represented a 'family' environment as did Morpheus' crew of the Nebuchadnezzar. This family atmosphere was most probably missing in The Matrix, as was shown by Anderson being lonely and depressed in the original Matrix before being shown and brought into the Matrix. Anderson however represents what can happen when one is on their own or isolated and lonely. It just happened that Zion was an alright place to be, but in real life, reality is not so kind and people, especially young people, can get caught up in the wrong crowd and end up sick, ill, disadvantaged, in vices and even dead. They call this there family but in actual fact it is not; it is like the anti-family. On first impressions, Morpheus and Trinity did not represent a healthy sort of people, or family environment, for example, their black outfits, dark demeanour and the club Anderson was taken to too meet Trinity in the original Matrix.

Morpheus represented a Father figure for Zion and Nebuchadnezzar. The rest of Zion and Nebuchadnezzar were like sons and daughters from various backgrounds, cultures and nationalities. These so called rebels of The Matrix were from different careers and backgrounds, as stated by one of the heads of Zion, Councillor Hamann. Agent Smith was trying to plead with Neo that there were things such as family and love in The Matrix, especially in their end fight, 'Why do you keeping fighting Mr. Anderson?...are you looking for love, for...'

Zion could have offered such things as family and love as well, and did represent freedom to an extent, but how long could these people be underground for, especially with a multiplying Zion population. Surely, they would have given in to an extent and wanted the freedoms of The Matrix, just like Cypher did in the original movie.

But it was what Zion represented, family and love in Zion as opposed to family and love in The Matrix that made its inhabitants and those new to it more wanting, if not needful, of it. Perhaps something could have been arranged with decision-makers or authorities of The Matrix to keep Zion and make it like a vacation or paradise away for people from The Matrix. Surely those in The Matrix should have acknowledged the importance and power of a place like Zion.

Like the need for love, the need for family was also evident and this highlights how something is missing in society in general, as well as in The Matrix and Zion, and can be filled spiritually, i.e. religion and or Heaven. But again, did the inhabitants of The Matrix and Zion even know of a Heaven, especially since they were grown, or were, as Agent Smith put it, crops. The machines in The Matrix are, in a weird sort of way, a family as well. Neo is shown to have some sort of connection with the machines, possibly making the machines his family as well. But those who are connected to The Matrix in the way Neo and the ships of Zion are, then the machines, or science and technology, are family to these 'plugged in' inhabitants of The Matrix.

Image

Anderson was a computer programmer from a top-level company, so he had a strong image. He was not dumb, but was in fact smart. However, his intelligence led him down the wrong track by getting into cyber-crime under the name of Neo, which he kept after meeting Morpheus and the crew. Anderson's cyber-crime was quite the opposite of his position and reputation as a computer programmer for a top company. Anderson seemed to relish his new role as Neo once he got going. However, what if Neo was not a smart person from a big company, but was in fact a simple sort of person with a simple profession like a Trades person. Jesus, for example, was the son of a carpenter, and Neo was almost compared to having a Christ-like influence on Zion and The Matrix. Anderson was sort of simple in a way, being reserved, quiet spoken and a bit of a loner.

Neo did not take to the image of The Matrix at first, as Morpheus stated to Neo and warned him, '...all I'm offering is the truth'. After seeing the levels upon levels of people being grown in The Matrix and after Morpheus had explained what The Matrix was to him, Neo's image of The Matrix made him flip out. This made Zion all the more attractive and appealing. Remember, this is a future-based, science fiction movie, and real life in everyday society is not like that. One thing about our society is that we have kept free of becoming too high-tech or science driven, for example, flying cars, but there are elements of it around with computers, Internet, phones, televisions and nuclear technology, and there has been mixed emotions with such science and technology, but this will be discussed under the theme of 'Technology and Science'.

Technology and Science

The Matrix oozes science and technology. Obviously, the movie is a future-based, science fiction film, but science and technology is still a big part of our current society, for example, energy use, communications, military, etc. The Action and being plugged into The Matrix, along with the information and experience it brings, would be quite an experience for those in Zion and certain people in The Matrix. This sort of technology was well advanced compared to what is available in our current society. But who would want to be part of The Matrix if that is what happens. As the saying goes, 'you can't have it given to you on a plate, you have to earn it'.

Information and experience being given this freely can make someone reckless and problematic. Hence, some struggle has to be there in real life on a healthy, structured and constructive level. Now it was a different case for Neo who was trying to save Zion, but The Matrix was a metaphor for science and technology and information going too far. Neo sat through 10 hours of information being installed into his head. That is a lot of information. This was a risk putting Neo up against the authorities with this amount of knowledge and power in him. Another person would not have done the same thing, but then again, not everyone was like Neo, nor had a task of saving Zion. The Matrix resembles Keanu Reeves other film, Johnny Neumonic, where he would store important in his brain which was like a hard drive.

4. Cast

Thomas Anderson/Neo

Thomas Anderson had one side of his life going for him in his career for a top computer company, but the other areas of his life were suffering with his family, social and love life. At least that is what is initially shown by the original movie. Thomas seemed bored, even lonely and depressed, resorting to cyber crime to pass his time and make a name for himself. Anderson wanted to know about The Matrix like so some others did, and this led him to Trinity and Morpheus. Perhaps Anderson was just lost and in having an idle mind resorted to going deeper into his life and that of the world's.

Interesting how Neo was in computers and he ended up becoming much like a computer himself, for example the hours he took to have the information installed in his head and the action he produced that followed. Anderson did not want to cooperate with authorities, so maybe this was his Neo-side coming out. But was finding out about the Matrix more important than bettering his current situation in life as Agent Smith had given him a chance?

It would have been difficult for Neo to accept the Matrix after Morpheus' explanation, especially having lived the way he did for so long. Additionally, and seeing the endless rows and levels where humans are grown, that would have really shaken Neo, or did it. It could have been a computer orgasm for Neo in that he was into computers, hence machines. It would have been interesting to get Neo's reaction to having all the information in his head. What was going through his mind to make the decisions he did, particularly with regards to his martial arts moves? Did he just make it up on the spot or was there a deeper train of thought? Perhaps Neo could have tried to match his knowledge and intelligence with the maker of the Matrix and come up with other options or solutions to this battle.

Morpheus

Morpheus was like a Father figure to those in Zion and the Nebuchadnezzar, with his guidance, wisdom, example and vigilance. He provided hope to those in Zion that someday Zion will be saved and they can go on living their lives in peace, safety and harmony. It would be interesting to see if Morpheus had tried a peaceful demonstration to initially save Zion, instead of resorting to violence. At least he was being honest in showing Neo the truth about the Matrix, taking the red pill or the blue pill. But what if Morpheus explained to Neo what the Matrix was before he put him through what he put him through? Would Neo have accepted Morpheus' offer?

It would have been a compliment to Neo that Morpheus thought he was The One. Being told he was The One definitely would have influenced Neo to say yes to Morpheus, but this could have come across as another mind game, for example Cypher. One would think Morpheus was on the same level as Neo, especially the way he talked and the example he gave. But despite being good, he was not as good as the Agents, which only Neo could match. Was Morpheus not improving and bettering himself because he thought Neo and or The One would do it all, or was he for real?

Trinity

Trinity was a beautiful woman in the Matrix. Cypher liked her, and it was understandable that Neo was going to like her too. It was like she was kept there just for Neo. It was interesting how she was named Trinity for a number of reasons. Firstly, Trinity's looks are mixed with dark hair, coloured eyes and fair skin. Secondly, her, Neo and Morpheus made up a Trinity-like set-up with each complimenting and needing each other. Was it Neo's influence and power that brought out the strength in Morpheus, Trinity and the people of Zion? Thirdly, Trinity had a threefold spirit in her, especially with her name, but that was yet to be proven. Agent Smith knew himself Trinity was a dangerous woman, as shown in the very first scenes of the original Matrix. Police squads were no match for Trinity, only the Agents were, and Trinity was really no match for them.

Agent Smith

What a powerful figure Agent Smith was. He had a relaxed, controlled and forthright presence. Smith gave Neo options to stay on the right track but he chose otherwise, for example, when first capturing him, just before fighting Neo after meeting The Oracle in Matrix Reloaded and the end fight with Neo in Matrix Reloaded. So Agent Smith did have a seemingly good side. At least he was trying to show, as a product himself of the Matrix that this was how the Matrix was, almost like people accepting the world around them. He could not see that Neo and the crew of Zion were fighting for a better cause.

After fighting Neo on the first few occasions, and finding he was getting nowhere, Agent Smith could have tried to strike a deal for Zion. Agent Smith, although looking like he was trying to do good, was not getting to the core issue of saving Zion and not trying to find it and destroy it, hence this is why Neo probably kept fighting. It was only when Neo talked with the maker, the Father of the Matrix that something was done; so Neo had to go past Agent Smith, a metaphor for the law, to get to a higher, in fact the highest authority in the maker of the Matrix. Could Agent Smith have been a son of the maker of the Matrix? Or made in his likeness or an element of his personality?

Instead, Agent Smith kept persisting trying to beat Neo, with a bit of pride in there, but in doing so, became the bad guy by trying to overtake people in the Matrix. He probably thought he was right so blindly that this is what he resorted to. Agent Smith was also a product of the Matrix, in fact, he was a high level of the law, so he would have aimed to keep fighting until his view was accepted.

Cypher

Cypher is like that likeable guy in the background, on the surface he is happy, but in this case, secretly he is sceptical and unbelieving. Morpheus did the same thing to Cypher, which he did to Neo, which he did to some in Zion, by releasing them from the Matrix. Cypher wants to believe but has given up believing, waiting all this time for something to happen and for The One to show his or her self. It would have been interesting to see Cypher's reaction to Morpheus once he told him what the Matrix was all about, after seeing Neo's reaction to it.

Yet, Cypher missed out on seeing Neo become The One near the end of the Matrix; talk about missing out. Cypher was like a Judas Escariot in Jesus' times by dobbing Morpheus and the crew of the Nebuchadnezzar into Agent Smith. Cypher was like the other guy in the picture who liked Trinity, apart from Neo. It is when Neo as The One came about that he saw a chance to let Trinity know he loved her. But Cypher had the chance to do this a long time ago, so why didn't he? Perhaps Morpheus said that Trinity is meant for The One, or Cypher did not act in time and was in fact intimidated by Neo – '...I didn't see you bringing me food'.

The Oracle

The Oracle was a happy, relaxed and wise female. Of course she was older, giving the connotation of wisdom. Having the children as The One hopefuls in the original Matrix, and baking cookies, showed a motherly presence. Perhaps this is motherly or family presence is what Neo missed in his life. The Oracle was also black, like Morpheus, possibly meaning how the black race also rule the world in various areas, like sport, music and dance and other areas, and are therefore a versatile race. It was through the Oracle that Neo found out someone liked him, '...I can see why she likes you'.

But this motherly belief was not enough to convince Neo he was the one. If the Oracle was the mother type, then Morpheus or the maker of the Matrix could have been the father type. Morpheus father for Zion, and the maker of the Matrix, father for the Matrix. It would have been interesting having the Oracle as Neo's long lost mother and the maker of the Matrix as Neo's long lost father; meaning how of course he was destined to be the One with such connections and blood-lines.

The maker-father of the Matrix

Of course he came into the movie towards the end of the series in the final instalment of the Matrix, Matrix Revolutions. It was interesting how the Oracle was black and the maker of the Matrix was white. Now of course people are different in general and within backgrounds and nationalities, but in this case, the Oracle stood for wisdom and love, and the maker of the Matrix stood for knowledge and power, '...it [the Matrix] was pure genius'. He was a very calm, reassuring and soft spoken person, and had an intelligent look and way about him; one might say of course being the creator of the Matrix. It took the creator of the Matrix to put some sense in Neo about the Matrix. Not even this important figure could have stopped Neo from saving and loving Trinity, pushing the limits to save her.

Merovingian & Persephone

This couple resembled Neo and Trinity, but would probably be classed as upper class. The Merovingian used to be like Neo, but whatever happened, it was like he was bought off and given a place in the Matrix. Some of his powers were shown with the use of the cake on the blonde girl and shifting Neo to somewhere in the mountains in an instant. Although he still had the love in him to an extent, his wife Persephone new Neo was like how the Merovingian used to be, and had the love there at that time. The Merovingian had become reckless in a way, and his wife Persephone acted the way she did because of this. She wanted that love back that the Merovingian used to have, and kissed Neo in a most passionate way as indicating his love as The One.

Perhaps this was a way for Merovingian and Persephone to renew and strengthen their relationship. The couple both looked attractive and powerful, sitting at the head table in the restaurant. In fact, this organisation made the scene look like they owned the restaurant or was like a wedding, possibly renewing their vows, just as Neo was to come on the scene.

Bane

Bane was a symbol that Agent Smith had taken his power to a new level, with his spirit overtaking another person, in this case Bane. Bane did look suspicious, possibly just awkward but it would have been hard to tell he was up to something, and that it was in fact Agent Smith. When Neo figured out Agent Smith was in Bane, he was in disbelief, realising the strength of Agent Smith and that of the Matrix. But was Neo disabled not being plugged into the Matrix, while Agent Smith looked to have all his powers? It is amazing those in authority in the Matrix did not do this sooner, trying to infiltrate Zion. That is how elusive those in Zion probably were, until Cypher handed over Morpheus to the Agents and forced out of him the location of Zion, '...we have their location, send in the sentinels'. Bane got very close to Zion by actually being inside, just what the Agents, and authorities in the Matrix, wanted.

5. Conclusion

According to Morpheus, Neo, or Anderson, made a perfect fit for being The One in the Matrix. Neo was a computer expert and interesting how the Matrix was a computer, and he was looking for and missing something in his life. Instead of combat training, which is always risky, diplomacy and people skills could have also been installed in Neo to negotiate with the authorities in the Matrix, especially the Agents, to save Zion. It is amazing the mind game Morpheus had to play with Neo to get him to be a part of the Matrix, yet not be a part of it. Perhaps Zion had its own Matrix-type set up for people to be in. It would have been good if Zion was saved and Neo and Trinity could have been like the Merovingian and Persephone and given a place in the Matrix or a similar place in Zion.

www.ingramcontent.com/pod-product-compliance
Lightning Source LLC
Chambersburg PA
CBHW081315180526
45170CB00007B/2717